SO YOU WANT TO WRITE A BOOK

AN INDIE AUTHOR GUIDE
TO OUTLINING AND PLANNING YOUR NEXT NOVEL

"Good books don't give up all their
secrets at once."
- Stephen King

"There is nothing to writing. All you do
is sit down at the typewriter and bleed."
- Ernest Hemingway

Table of Contents

Introduction

I'm an author… an indie-author to be exact. I don't have a huge advance from some fancy publishing house that I'm living on while I sit in a cottage somewhere in the woods pecking away at the keyboard of my old-fashioned typewriter. Don't get me wrong, I wouldn't turn that down—well, maybe the typewriter, but I don't have it yet. If you're looking for advice from someone who has already made it big like Stephen King (my personal role model), James Patterson, Danielle Steel, Richelle Mead, Rachel Caine, or any other New York Times best seller, then my advice is to find a good agent – one who specializes in the genre you want to write in. However, if you're just looking to start your first novel, or even your tenth, and you want some advice from someone like you, someone with a passion for writing, who still finds joy in the discovery of new characters, then you've come to the right place.

I published my first book, a compilation of poetry in 2008. No, it didn't sell. In my experience, poetry never sells until the poet is long dead. Since then, my writing style has changed drastically and my story telling abilities have gotten much better-at least that's what my kids say. Since 2012, I have published six fiction novels (4 in the Blood Angel Series and 2 in the Sector C Series), with another one coming late 2017. What does that mean about my qualifications for guiding you on your journey to finishing your fiction novel? Not much, other than the fact that I've been there… I've done it. Maybe you can learn from some of my mistakes along the way, and use some of the tools I've developed that have made my process easier.

AUTHOR –

1. The writer of a literary work (such as a book)
2. One that originates or creates something: software authors, film authors, the author of this crime

Author. 2011. In Merriam-Webster.com. Retrieved October 4, 2017, from https://www.merriam-webster.com/dictionary/author

---

INDIE-AUTHOR –

"Being an indie author is primarily an approach to writing and publishing, a matter of self-definition. If you see yourself as the creative director of your books, from concept to completion and beyond, then you're indie."

Ross, O. (June 18, 2013) What IS An Indie Author? Retrieved from https://selfpublishingadvice.org

---

BLOOD ANGEL SERIES –

Awaken (book 1) published 2012
Beginnings (book 2) published 2013
Revenge (book 3) published 2014
Pursuit (book 4) published 2016

SECTOR C SERIES –

The Chosen (book 1) published 2015
The Hunted (book 2) published 2015
The Truth (book 3) published 2017

How to Use this Guide

The concept of a self-help guide isn't a new one, and trust me there are plenty of them out there to help you write a book. I could ask why you picked this one up, but it doesn't matter if it was the cover, the blurb on the back, someone recommend it, or you just felt compelled. The point is, you're here and I'm glad you are.

You could just sit down at your computer and start typing. That's how I started my first novel. A lot of authors, especially those of us indie-authors, start out that way. What you might not know is we also end up deleting a lot of our hard work because either the plot is going nowhere, the characters aren't interesting, or we get lost in the story and can't find our way to the end.

TIP –
Use pencil… you'll be doing a lot of brainstorming and you'll probably want to revise your work as you go. Each exercise is going to help you understand your story and your characters better, so don't be afraid to go back and make changes.

My goal is to help you avoid as many of the painful, time-consuming mistakes as I can. How am I going to do that? By providing easy to complete worksheets to help you outline and plan your story from start to finish. No, you're not going to write your novel within these pages, there isn't enough room for that, but you will be developing the skeleton outline that will eventually become your novel. Just complete each task and use the information you create here while typing your novel in word. Yes, you could use a novel writing software like Scrivener, Ulysses, EasyWriter, Evernote, or FocusWriter, but my recommendation is good old Microsoft Word. Most people already have Microsoft Word on their home computer and it's easy to use. Just open and start typing. Formatting your manuscript comes later, once you actually have a manuscript, so don't worry about it while you write, just get your story on paper.

<u>What is Your Novel About?</u>

The Art of the One-Sentence Summary

Ok, so it probably doesn't sound all that hard to write a single sentence, does it? But the truth is, this one little sentence is extremely important. It will serve as your pitch line – your ten second pitch to get people interested in hearing more, so it has to be good. Basically, it is your entire novel wrapped up into one short, gripping sentence. The hard part is not saying too much. Keep it under twenty words, and focus on the big picture plot as well as the struggle of your main character. *HINT: Check out the New York Times Best Sellers list to read some great examples of one-sentence summaries.*

Now, practice your one-sentence summary!

Completed one-sentence summary:

The Art of the One-Paragraph Summary

Ok, now we're going to expand on that amazing one-sentence summary you've already completed. Your paragraph summary is going to be a big picture overview of your story and should give us an idea of the setting of the story as well as the struggles or obstacles your main character will face and of course the ending. This paragraph should be broken down as follows:

- Sentence one – Set up the story
- Sentence two – Obstacle #1
- Sentence three – Obstacle #2
- Sentence four – Obstacle #3
- Sentence five – closing (end of the story)

The point of developing a one-paragraph summary is to help keep your writing on track. If you know the obstacles your main character will face, and in what order, then you'll be able to guide your writing toward those events.

Now let's work on developing your paragraph:

Where does your story take place?

____

____

____

Describe obstacle #1:

____

____

____

Describe obstacle #2:

____

____

____

Describe obstacle #3:

____

____

____

How does the story end for your main character?

____

____

____

Completed one-paragraph summary:

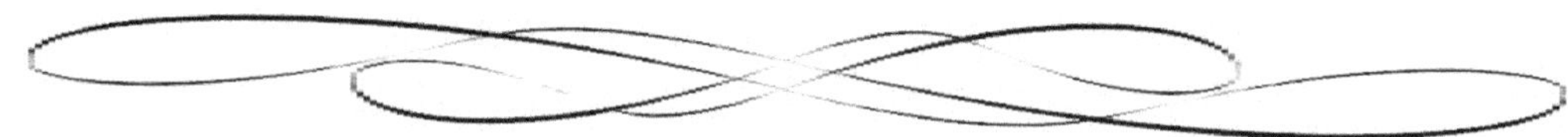

"Plot is no more than footprints left in the snow after your characters have run by on their way to incredible destinations."
- Ray Bradbury

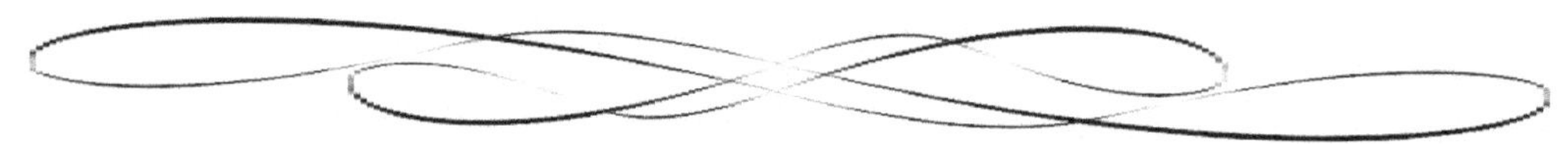

Planning Your Plot

You don't have to know exactly where your story will take you, what will happen to your characters, or even the ending… not yet anyway. However, if you're going to write a novel, or even a novella, you will need to have a strong understanding of the stories plot. How it plays out, and the adventure it takes you on, may change as you go but without a clear picture of the general plot you could easily get lost in the quicksand of writing.

Use the following plot planning format to help develop a clear understanding of your stories plot! You may need more than one completed plot planning worksheets – depending on the number of crisis in your story. I've included four on the following pages.

1. **Exposition** – Give the background information about setting and characters.
2. **Rising Action A.** – Describe the character
3. **Rising Action B**. – Describe the character's crisis
4. **Rising Action C.** – New conflict/character crisis worsens
5. **Climax** – Character crisis peaks! This is the most intense part of the story (or the act – depending on how many crises you are planning).
6. **Falling Action A.** – Begin resolving the character crisis
7. **Falling Action B.** – Crisis is solved. This doesn't have to mean a happy Hollywood ending.
8. **Resolution** – Tie up loose ends and conclude (If this is the last crisis of the story).

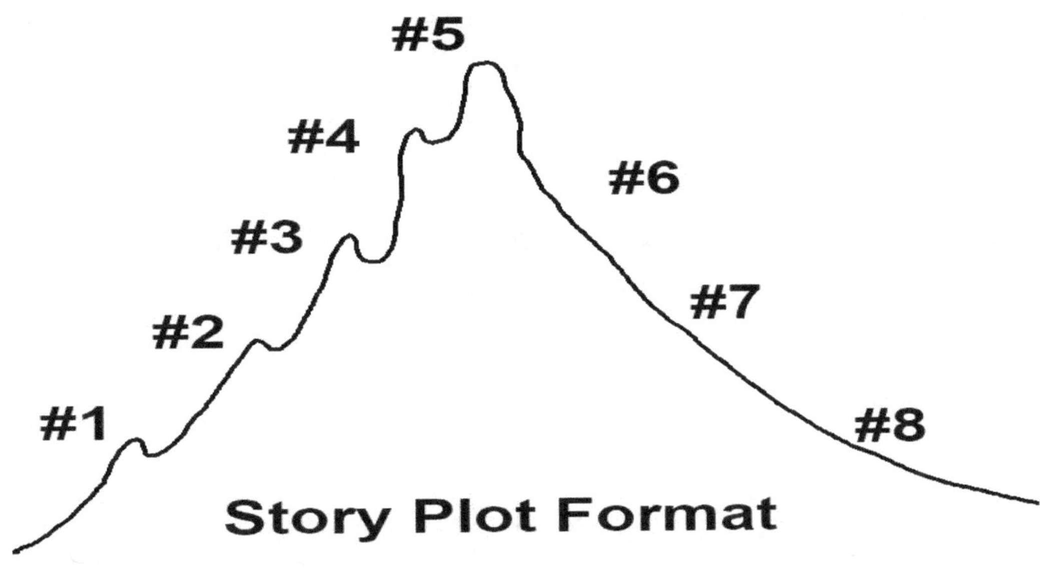

STORY PLOT WORKSHEET #1

5. Climax

4. Rising Action C.

6. Falling Action A.

3. Rising Action B.

7. Falling Action B.

2. Rising Action A.

8. Resolution

1. Exposition

STORY PLOT WORKSHEET #2

5. Climax

4. Rising Action C.

6. Falling Action A.

3. Rising Action B.

7. Falling Action B.

2. Rising Action A.

8. Resolution

2. Exposition

5. Climax

4. Rising Action C.

6. Falling Action A.

3. Rising Action B.

7. Falling Action B.

2. Rising Action A.

8. Resolution

3. Exposition

5. Climax

4. Rising Action C.

6. Falling Action A.

3. Rising Action B.

7. Falling Action B.

2. Rising Action A.

8. Resolution

4. Exposition

"I always have a basic plot outline, but
I like to leave some things to be decided
while I write."
- J.K. Rowling

Skeleton Outline

If you've ever read, seen, or been in a play then this next step should be pretty easy for you. Think of your skeleton outline as a three-act play. In act 1 we get the background, understand the setting, meet the main characters, and encounter the first obstacle. The second obstacle happens near the middle of act 2 and the third obstacle happens at the end of act 2. Both obstacle 2 and 3 should be related to obstacle 1. Think of them as the results of the main character trying to fix what happened with obstacle 1. Act 3 is when everything gets worked out and the story is wrapped up. Keep in mind, when I say "worked out" I don't mean your story has to have a Hollywood ending – that is completely up to you.

Now, let's break down your three acts!

ACT 1

Background Notes	
Setting	
Obstacle #1	

Main Character's reaction to Obstacle #1	
Obstacle #2	
Main Character's Reaction to Obstacle #2	
Obstacle #3	

Main Character's Reaction to Obstacle #3	
Wrap-up/ Conclusion	

Additional Notes:

"I try to create sympathy for my characters, then turn the monsters loose."
- Stephen King

Character Development

To talk about character development, first you must understand the different types of characters you might encounter throughout your novel. Since my background is in theatre and film as an actress, I like to look at my characters through the eye of a film lens.

For this section we are going to look at the Star Wars movies, mainly episodes IV, V, and VI, to help explain the most common character types. If you haven't seen the original Star Wars movies, shame on you! No, but seriously, if you haven't seen them, do it now!

Use the descriptions and examples below to come up with your own examples for each character type. Your examples can be from literature, television, or film—this is just practice. Then, using the worksheet, describe each of these characters as you see them within your story.

Understanding Character Types

8 Most Common Character Types:

- **Protagonist** – This is the good character in your story – often your main character—your hero. This will be the "victim" or main target of the antagonist.

  Star Wars Example: Luke Skywalker

  Additional Examples: ____

- **Antagonist** – This is the character who antagonizes (hence the name antagonist) the other characters in the story. This is NOT a nice character.

  Star Wars Example: Darth Vader

  Additional Examples: ____

- **Confidante** – This is the character with whom your protagonist confides in. The best friend, the guy next door, the favorite pet, the dead parent, the mentor… you get the picture. This character helps you reveal the main character's personality, thoughts, intentions, etc. without just telling the reader what you feel they need to know.

  Star Wars Example: Ben (Obi-Wan) Kenobi and then Jedi Master Yoda

  Additional Examples: ____

- **Foil Characters** – these characters are used to enhance another character through contrast. Think of the good cop/bad cop scenario. Although not always, the foil character can be the same as the antagonist.

  Star Wars Example: Both Darth Vader and Hon Solo fit this role. Darth Vader, much like Luke Skywalker is very powerful in the way of the force, but they are a clear contrast to one another as Darth Vader uses his power for evil and Luke uses his for good. Hon Solo is seen as a foil character simply because his personality traits; charming, charismatic, rebellious, etc. are in direct contrast to Luke's somewhat awkward innocents.

Additional Examples: ____

- **Developing Character** – This character goes through some type of change in personality, belief, etc. throughout the course of the story.

  Star Wars Example: If you look at all of the Star Wars film, Anakin Skywalker is clearly a developing character. He starts out as this young innocent boy, grows into a powerful Jedi, and then – spoiler alert – turns to the dark side and becomes the stories main Antagonist (Darth Vader).

  Additional Examples: ____

- **Flat Characters** – This will often be smaller supporting characters or extras. You only learn one or two things about these characters' personalities throughout the story and they don't change.

  Star Wars Example: An example of this character type would be the Stormtroopers. We never learn anything about them and they are more of a collective than individual characters.

  Additional Examples: ____

- **Static Character** – Much like the flat characters, the static characters don't change throughout the story. Their outlook, motivation, and personality stays the same. However, these characters may be more developed, revealing more about themselves throughout the story, than a flat character would be.

  Star Wars Example: C-3PO, R2-D2, and Chewbacca. These characters, however vital to the story, don't really change throughout the story.

  Additional Examples: ____

- **Stock Character** – These are stereotypical characters that you can recognize right away when reading a story or watching a movie. These characters are not the focus of the story and are definitely not developed throughout the story. This is the guy in the horror film that goes out to see what made the weird noise and ends up dying first.

  Star Wars Example: Any number of the X-wing starfighter pilots who were part of the Red Squadron in the Rebel Alliance that were killed during the Battle of Yavin.

  Additional Examples: ____

Character Profile Worksheets

Below you will find 10 Character Profile Worksheets – you may need them all or you may find only a few are necessary.

Character #1 Name: ____

PICK ONE

___ Protagonist

___ Antagonist

___ Supporting Character

BASIC STATISTICS CHARACTER #1

Name: ____

Age: ____

Nationality: ____

Socioeconomic Level as a child: ___________________________________

Socioeconomic Level as an adult: __________________________________

Hometown: ____

Occupation: ____

Talents/Skills: ____

Siblings (describe relationship): ___________________________________

____

____

Spouse (describe relationship): ____________________________________

Children (describe relationship): ___________________________________

____

____

Grandparents (describe relationship): _______________________________

____

____

Grandchildren (describe relationship): ______________________________

____

____

Significant Others (describe relationship): ___________________________

____

____

Relationship skills: ____

PHYSICAL CHARACTERISTICS:

Height: ____

Weight: ____

Race: ____

Eye Color: ____

Hair Color: ____

Glasses or contact lenses? ____________________________

Skin color: ____

Shape of Face: ____

Distinguishing features: ______________________________

How does he/she dress? ________________________________

Mannerisms: ____

Habits (smoking, drinking etc.): ______________________

Health: ____

Hobbies: ____

Favorite Sayings: _____________________________________

Disabilities: ____

Style: ____

INTELLECTUAL/MENTAL/PERSONALITY ATTRIBUTES AND ATTITUDES

Educational Background: ________________________________

Any Mental Illnesses? _________________________________

Character's short-term goals in life: _________________

Character's long-term goals in life: __________________

How does Character see himself/herself? _______________

____

How does Character believe he/she is perceived by others? _______________

____

How self-confident is the character? __________________

Does the character seem ruled by emotion or logic or some combination thereof? _________

____

____

EMOTIONAL CHARACTERISTICS

Strengths/Weaknesses: ____
Introvert or Extrovert? ____
How does the character deal with anger? ________________________________
With sadness? ____
With conflict? ____
With change? ____
With loss? ____
What would the character change about him/her-self? _____________________
What motivates this character? ____
What are this character's main personality traits? ________________________

____

____

____

SPIRITUAL CHARACTERISTICS

Does the character believe in God? _____________________________________
What are the character's spiritual beliefs? _______________________________
Is religion or spirituality a part of this character's life? ____________________
If so, what role does it play? ____

How the Character is Involved in the Story

Character's role in the novel (main character? hero? heroine? Romantic interest? etc.):

____

Scene where character first appears: ____________________________________

____

Relationships with other characters: (Describe relationship with the following characters)
1. *Name*: _____________________________ *Relationship*: ________________

____

____

2. *Name*: _____________________________ *Relationship*: ________________

____

3. *Name*: _________________________ *Relationship*: _________________________

____

4. *Name*: _________________________ *Relationship*: _________________________

____

5. *Name*: _________________________ *Relationship*: _________________________

____

How is this character different at the end of the novel from when the novel began:

____

____

____

____

____

____

Additional Notes on This Character:

____

____

____

____

____

____

____

Character Profile Worksheet

Character #2 Name: _______________________________________

BASIC STATISTICS CHARACTER #2

Name: ____

Age: ____

Nationality: ____

Socioeconomic Level as a child: _________________________________

Socioeconomic Level as an adult: ________________________________

Hometown: ____

Occupation: ____

Talents/Skills: ____

Siblings (describe relationship): ________________________________

____

____

Spouse (describe relationship): _________________________________

Children (describe relationship): ________________________________

____

____

Grandparents (describe relationship): ___________________________

____

____

Grandchildren (describe relationship): ___________________________

____

____

Significant Others (describe relationship): _______________________

____

____

Relationship skills: ____

PHYSICAL CHARACTERISTICS:

Height: ____

Weight: ____

Race: _______________

Eye Color: _______________

Hair Color: _______________

Glasses or contact lenses? _______________

Skin color: _______________

Shape of Face: _______________

Distinguishing features: _______________

How does he/she dress? _______________

Mannerisms: _______________

Habits (smoking, drinking etc.): _______________

Health: _______________

Hobbies: _______________

Favorite Sayings: _______________

Disabilities: _______________

Style: _______________

INTELLECTUAL/MENTAL/PERSONALITY ATTRIBUTES AND ATTITUDES

Educational Background: _______________

Any Mental Illnesses? _______________

Character's short-term goals in life: _______________

Character's long-term goals in life: _______________

How does Character see himself/herself? _______________

How does Character believe he/she is perceived by others? _______________

How self-confident is the character? _______________

Does the character seem ruled by emotion or logic or some combination thereof? _______________

EMOTIONAL CHARACTERISTICS

Strengths/Weaknesses: _______________

Introvert or Extrovert? _______________

How does the character deal with anger? _______________

With sadness? ____
With conflict? ____
With change? ____
With loss? ____
What would the character change about him/her-self? ____________________
What motivates this character? ____
What are this character's main personality traits? ______________________
____
____
____

SPIRITUAL CHARACTERISTICS

Does the character believe in God? ____________________________________
What are the character's spiritual beliefs? ______________________________
Is religion or spirituality a part of this character's life? ________________
If so, what role does it play? ____

How the Character is Involved in the Story

Character's role in the novel (main character? hero? heroine? Romantic interest? etc.):

____
Scene where character first appears: __________________________________
____
____
Relationships with other characters: (Describe relationship with the following characters)
1. *Name*: ______________________ *Relationship*: ______________________
____
____

2. *Name*: ______________________ *Relationship*: ______________________
____
____

3. *Name*: ______________________ *Relationship*: ______________________

4. *Name*: _______________________ *Relationship*: _______________________

5. *Name*: _______________________ *Relationship*: _______________________

How is this character different at the end of the novel from when the novel began:

Additional Notes on This Character:

Character Profile Worksheet

PICK ONE

____ Protagonist

____ Antagonist

____ Supporting Character

Character #3 Name: _______________________________________

BASIC STATISTICS CHARACTER #3

Name: ____

Age: ____

Nationality: ____

Socioeconomic Level as a child: ____________________________

Socioeconomic Level as an adult: ___________________________

Hometown: ____

Occupation: ____

Talents/Skills: ____

Siblings (describe relationship): ___________________________

____

____

Spouse (describe relationship): ____________________________

Children (describe relationship): ___________________________

____

____

Grandparents (describe relationship): _______________________

____

____

Grandchildren (describe relationship): ______________________

____

____

Significant Others (describe relationship): ___________________

____

____

Relationship skills: ______________________________________

PHYSICAL CHARACTERISTICS:

Height: ____

Weight: ____

Race: ____

Eye Color: ____

Hair Color: ____

Glasses or contact lenses? __________________________________

Skin color: ____

Shape of Face: ____

Distinguishing features: ____________________________________

How does he/she dress? ______________________________________

Mannerisms: ____

Habits (smoking, drinking etc.): ____________________________

Health: ____

Hobbies: ____

Favorite Sayings: ____

Disabilities: ____

Style: ____

INTELLECTUAL/MENTAL/PERSONALITY ATTRIBUTES AND ATTITUDES

Educational Background: ______________________________________

Any Mental Illnesses? _______________________________________

Character's short-term goals in life: _______________________

Character's long-term goals in life: ________________________

How does Character see himself/herself? _____________________
____

How does Character believe he/she is perceived by others? ___
____

How self-confident is the character? ________________________

Does the character seem ruled by emotion or logic or some combination thereof? _______
____
____

EMOTIONAL CHARACTERISTICS

Strengths/Weaknesses: _______________________________________

Introvert or Extrovert? _____________________________________

How does the character deal with anger? _____________________

With sadness? ____

With conflict? ____

With change? ____

With loss? ____

What would the character change about him/her-self? _______________________________

What motivates this character? ____

What are this character's main personality traits? __________________________________

____

____

____

SPIRITUAL CHARACTERISTICS

Does the character believe in God? ____

What are the character's spiritual beliefs? ____

Is religion or spirituality a part of this character's life? ______________________________

If so, what role does it play? ____

How the Character is Involved in the Story

Character's role in the novel (main character? hero? heroine? Romantic interest? etc.):

____

Scene where character first appears: ____

____

____

Relationships with other characters: (Describe relationship with the following characters)

1. *Name*: ____________________________ *Relationship*: ___________________________

____

____

2. *Name*: ____________________________ *Relationship*: ___________________________

____

____

3. *Name*: ____________________________ *Relationship*: ___________________________

4. *Name*: _________________________ *Relationship*: _____________________

5. *Name*: _________________________ *Relationship*: _____________________

How is this character different at the end of the novel from when the novel began:

Additional Notes on This Character:

Character Profile Worksheet

PICK ONE

___ Protagonist

___ Antagonist

___ Supporting Character

Character #4 Name: _______________________________________

BASIC STATISTICS CHARACTER #4

Name: _______________________________________

Age: _______________________________________

Nationality: _______________________________________

Socioeconomic Level as a child: _______________________

Socioeconomic Level as an adult: _______________________

Hometown: _______________________________________

Occupation: _______________________________________

Talents/Skills: _______________________________________

Siblings (describe relationship): _______________________

____

____

Spouse (describe relationship): _______________________

Children (describe relationship): _______________________

____

____

Grandparents (describe relationship): _______________________

____

____

Grandchildren (describe relationship): _______________________

____

____

Significant Others (describe relationship): _______________________

____

____

Relationship skills: _______________________________________

PHYSICAL CHARACTERISTICS:

Height: _______________________________________

Weight: _______________________________________

Race: ____

Eye Color: ____

Hair Color: ____

Glasses or contact lenses? ____

Skin color: ____

Shape of Face: ____

Distinguishing features: ____

How does he/she dress? ____

Mannerisms: ____

Habits (smoking, drinking etc.): ____

Health: ____

Hobbies: ____

Favorite Sayings: ____

Disabilities: ____

Style: ____

INTELLECTUAL/MENTAL/PERSONALITY ATTRIBUTES AND ATTITUDES

Educational Background: ____

Any Mental Illnesses? ____

Character's short-term goals in life: ____

Character's long-term goals in life: ____

How does Character see himself/herself? ____

How does Character believe he/she is perceived by others? ____

How self-confident is the character? ____

Does the character seem ruled by emotion or logic or some combination thereof? ____

EMOTIONAL CHARACTERISTICS

Strengths/Weaknesses: ____

Introvert or Extrovert? ____

How does the character deal with anger? ____

With sadness? ____

With conflict? ____

With change? ____

With loss? ____

What would the character change about him/her-self? ___________________________

What motivates this character? ____

What are this character's main personality traits? _____________________________

____

____

____

SPIRITUAL CHARACTERISTICS

Does the character believe in God? ____

What are the character's spiritual beliefs? ______________________________________

Is religion or spirituality a part of this character's life? __________________________

If so, what role does it play? ____

How the Character is Involved in the Story

Character's role in the novel (main character? hero? heroine? Romantic interest? etc.):

____

Scene where character first appears: ____

____

Relationships with other characters: (Describe relationship with the following characters)

1. *Name*: ____________________________ *Relationship*: _______________________

____

____

2. *Name*: ____________________________ *Relationship*: _______________________

____

____

3. *Name*: ____________________________ *Relationship*: _______________________

4. *Name*: _______________________________ *Relationship*: _______________________________

5. *Name*: _______________________________ *Relationship*: _______________________________

How is this character different at the end of the novel from when the novel began:

Additional Notes on This Character:

Character Profile Worksheet

<table>
<tr><td>

Character #5 Name: _________________________________

BASIC STATISTICS CHARACTER #5

</td><td>

PICK ONE

___ Protagonist

___ Antagonist

___ Supporting Character

</td></tr>
</table>

Name: ____

Age: ____

Nationality: ____

Socioeconomic Level as a child: _____________________________

Socioeconomic Level as an adult: ___________________________

Hometown: ____

Occupation: ____

Talents/Skills: _______________________________________

Siblings (describe relationship): ____________________________

____

____

Spouse (describe relationship): _____________________________

Children (describe relationship): ____________________________

____

____

Grandparents (describe relationship): _______________________

____

____

Grandchildren (describe relationship): ______________________

____

____

Significant Others (describe relationship): ___________________

____

____

Relationship skills: ____________________________________

PHYSICAL CHARACTERISTICS:

Height: ____

Weight: ____

Race: _______________________________________

Eye Color: _______________________________________

Hair Color: _______________________________________

Glasses or contact lenses? _______________________________________

Skin color: _______________________________________

Shape of Face: _______________________________________

Distinguishing features: _______________________________________

How does he/she dress? _______________________________________

Mannerisms: _______________________________________

Habits (smoking, drinking etc.): _______________________________________

Health: _______________________________________

Hobbies: _______________________________________

Favorite Sayings: _______________________________________

Disabilities: _______________________________________

Style: _______________________________________

INTELLECTUAL/MENTAL/PERSONALITY ATTRIBUTES AND ATTITUDES

Educational Background: _______________________________________

Any Mental Illnesses? _______________________________________

Character's short-term goals in life: _______________________________________

Character's long-term goals in life: _______________________________________

How does Character see himself/herself? _______________________________________

____

How does Character believe he/she is perceived by others? _______________________________________

____

How self-confident is the character? _______________________________________

Does the character seem ruled by emotion or logic or some combination thereof? _______________________________________

____

____

EMOTIONAL CHARACTERISTICS

Strengths/Weaknesses: _______________________________________

Introvert or Extrovert? _______________________________________

How does the character deal with anger? _______________________________________

With sadness? ____

With conflict? ____

With change? ____

With loss? ____

What would the character change about him/her-self? ___________________________

What motivates this character? ____

What are this character's main personality traits? ______________________________

____

____

____

SPIRITUAL CHARACTERISTICS

Does the character believe in God? ____

What are the character's spiritual beliefs? ______________________________________

Is religion or spirituality a part of this character's life? __________________________

If so, what role does it play? ____

How the Character is Involved in the Story

Character's role in the novel (main character? hero? heroine? Romantic interest? etc.):

____

Scene where character first appears: ____

____

____

Relationships with other characters: (Describe relationship with the following characters)

1. *Name*: _______________________ *Relationship*: ____________________________

____

____

2. *Name*: _______________________ *Relationship*: ____________________________

____

____

3. *Name*: _______________________ *Relationship*: ____________________________

4. Name: _________________________ _Relationship_: _________________________

5. Name: _________________________ _Relationship_: _________________________

How is this character different at the end of the novel from when the novel began:

Additional Notes on This Character:

Character Profile Worksheet

PICK ONE

___ Protagonist

___ Antagonist

___ Supporting Character

Character #6 Name: _______________________________________

BASIC STATISTICS CHARACTER #6

Name: ____

Age: ____

Nationality: ____

Socioeconomic Level as a child: ____________________________

Socioeconomic Level as an adult: ___________________________

Hometown: ____

Occupation: ____

Talents/Skills: ____

Siblings (describe relationship): ___________________________

____

____

Spouse (describe relationship): ____________________________

Children (describe relationship): ___________________________

____

____

Grandparents (describe relationship): _______________________

____

____

Grandchildren (describe relationship): ______________________

____

____

Significant Others (describe relationship): ___________________

____

____

Relationship skills: ______________________________________

PHYSICAL CHARACTERISTICS:

Height: ____

Weight: ____

Race: ____

Eye Color: _______________________________________

Hair Color: _______________________________________

Glasses or contact lenses? _______________________

Skin color: _______________________________________

Shape of Face: ___________________________________

Distinguishing features: _________________________

How does he/she dress? ___________________________

Mannerisms: _______________________________________

Habits (smoking, drinking etc.): _________________

Health: ____

Hobbies: ____

Favorite Sayings: ________________________________

Disabilities: ____________________________________

Style: ____

INTELLECTUAL/MENTAL/PERSONALITY ATTRIBUTES AND ATTITUDES

Educational Background: __________________________

Any Mental Illnesses? ____________________________

Character's short-term goals in life: ____________

Character's long-term goals in life: _____________

How does Character see himself/herself? __________

____

How does Character believe he/she is perceived by others? _______

____

How self-confident is the character? _____________

Does the character seem ruled by emotion or logic or some combination thereof? _______

____

____

EMOTIONAL CHARACTERISTICS

Strengths/Weaknesses: ____________________________

Introvert or Extrovert? __________________________

How does the character deal with anger? __________

With sadness? ____
With conflict? ____
With change? ____
With loss? ____
What would the character change about him/her-self? _______________________
What motivates this character? ____
What are this character's main personality traits? _________________________

____
____
____

SPIRITUAL CHARACTERISTICS

Does the character believe in God? _____________________________________
What are the character's spiritual beliefs? ________________________________
Is religion or spirituality a part of this character's life? ____________________
If so, what role does it play? ____

How the Character is Involved in the Story

Character's role in the novel (main character? hero? heroine? Romantic interest? etc.):

____
Scene where character first appears: ____________________________________

____
____
Relationships with other characters: (Describe relationship with the following characters)
1. *Name*: _______________________ *Relationship*: _______________________

____
____

2. *Name*: _______________________ *Relationship*: _______________________

____
____

3. *Name*: _______________________ *Relationship*: _______________________

____

____

4. *Name*: _______________________ *Relationship*: _______________

____

____

5. *Name*: _______________________ *Relationship*: _______________

____

____

How is this character different at the end of the novel from when the novel began:

____

____

____

____

____

____

____

Additional Notes on This Character:

____

____

____

____

____

____

____

____

____

Character Profile Worksheet

<table><tr><td>PICK ONE</td></tr><tr><td>___ Protagonist</td></tr><tr><td>___ Antagonist</td></tr><tr><td>___ Supporting Character</td></tr></table>

Character #7 Name: _______________________________________

BASIC STATISTICS CHARACTER #7

Name: _______________________________________

Age: _______________________________________

Nationality: _______________________________________

Socioeconomic Level as a child: _______________________

Socioeconomic Level as an adult: ______________________

Hometown: _______________________________________

Occupation: _______________________________________

Talents/Skills: _______________________________________

Siblings (describe relationship): ______________________

____

____

Spouse (describe relationship): ________________________

Children (describe relationship): ______________________

____

____

Grandparents (describe relationship): __________________

____

____

Grandchildren (describe relationship): _________________

____

____

Significant Others (describe relationship): ____________

____

____

Relationship skills: ___________________________________

PHYSICAL CHARACTERISTICS:

Height: _______________________________________

Weight: _______________________________________

Race: ____

Eye Color: ____

Hair Color: ____

Glasses or contact lenses? ____

Skin color: ____

Shape of Face: ____

Distinguishing features: ____

How does he/she dress? ____

Mannerisms: ____

Habits (smoking, drinking etc.): ____

Health: ____

Hobbies: ____

Favorite Sayings: ____

Disabilities: ____

Style: ____

INTELLECTUAL/MENTAL/PERSONALITY ATTRIBUTES AND ATTITUDES

Educational Background: ____

Any Mental Illnesses? ____

Character's short-term goals in life: ____

Character's long-term goals in life: ____

How does Character see himself/herself? ____
____

How does Character believe he/she is perceived by others? ____
____

How self-confident is the character? ____

Does the character seem ruled by emotion or logic or some combination thereof? ____
____
____

EMOTIONAL CHARACTERISTICS

Strengths/Weaknesses: ____

Introvert or Extrovert? ____

How does the character deal with anger? ____

With sadness? ____
With conflict? ____
With change? ____
With loss? ____
What would the character change about him/her-self? ___________________
What motivates this character? ___________________________________
What are this character's main personality traits? ___________________

____
____
____

SPIRITUAL CHARACTERISTICS

Does the character believe in God? _________________________________
What are the character's spiritual beliefs? ___________________________
Is religion or spirituality a part of this character's life? _______________
If so, what role does it play? ____________________________________

How the Character is Involved in the Story

Character's role in the novel (main character? hero? heroine? Romantic interest? etc.):

____
Scene where character first appears: _______________________________
____
____

Relationships with other characters: (Describe relationship with the following characters)
1. *Name*: _____________________ *Relationship*: _________________

____
____

2. *Name*: _____________________ *Relationship*: _________________

____
____

3. *Name*: _____________________ *Relationship*: _________________

4. *Name*: ________________________ *Relationship*: ________________________

5. *Name*: ________________________ *Relationship*: ________________________

How is this character different at the end of the novel from when the novel began:

Additional Notes on This Character:

Character Profile Worksheet

Character #8 Name: _______________________________

BASIC STATISTICS CHARACTER #8

Name: _______________________________

Age: _______________________________

Nationality: _______________________________

Socioeconomic Level as a child: _______________________________

Socioeconomic Level as an adult: _______________________________

Hometown: _______________________________

Occupation: _______________________________

Talents/Skills: _______________________________

Siblings (describe relationship): _______________________________

____

____

Spouse (describe relationship): _______________________________

Children (describe relationship): _______________________________

____

____

Grandparents (describe relationship): _______________________________

____

____

Grandchildren (describe relationship): _______________________________

____

____

Significant Others (describe relationship): _______________________________

____

____

Relationship skills: _______________________________

PHYSICAL CHARACTERISTICS:

Height: _______________________________

Weight: _______________________________

Race: ____

Eye Color: ____

Hair Color: ____

Glasses or contact lenses? ____

Skin color: ____

Shape of Face: ____

Distinguishing features: ____

How does he/she dress? ____

Mannerisms: ____

Habits (smoking, drinking etc.): ____

Health: ____

Hobbies: ____

Favorite Sayings: ____

Disabilities: ____

Style: ____

INTELLECTUAL/MENTAL/PERSONALITY ATTRIBUTES AND ATTITUDES

Educational Background: ____

Any Mental Illnesses? ____

Character's short-term goals in life: ____

Character's long-term goals in life: ____

How does Character see himself/herself? ____

____

How does Character believe he/she is perceived by others? ____

____

How self-confident is the character? ____

Does the character seem ruled by emotion or logic or some combination thereof? _______________

____

____

EMOTIONAL CHARACTERISTICS

Strengths/Weaknesses: ____

Introvert or Extrovert? ____

How does the character deal with anger? ____

With sadness? ____

With conflict? ____

With change? ____

With loss? ____

What would the character change about him/her-self? _______________________

What motivates this character? _______________________________________

What are this character's main personality traits? _______________________

____

____

____

SPIRITUAL CHARACTERISTICS

Does the character believe in God? _______________________________________

What are the character's spiritual beliefs? _______________________________

Is religion or spirituality a part of this character's life? _________________

If so, what role does it play? _______________________________________

How the Character is Involved in the Story

Character's role in the novel (main character? hero? heroine? Romantic interest? etc.):

____

Scene where character first appears: _______________________________________

____

Relationships with other characters: (Describe relationship with the following characters)

1. *Name*: _______________________ *Relationship*: _______________________

____

____

2. *Name*: _______________________ *Relationship*: _______________________

____

____

3. *Name*: _______________________ *Relationship*: _______________________

____

____

4. *Name*: _____________________________ *Relationship*: _____________________

____

____

5. *Name*: _____________________________ *Relationship*: _____________________

____

____

How is this character different at the end of the novel from when the novel began:

____

____

____

____

____

____

____

Additional Notes on This Character:

____

____

____

____

____

____

____

____

____

Character Profile Worksheet

<table>
<tr><td>PICK ONE</td></tr>
<tr><td>____ Protagonist</td></tr>
<tr><td>____ Antagonist</td></tr>
<tr><td>____ Supporting Character</td></tr>
</table>

Character #9 Name: ____

BASIC STATISTICS CHARACTER #9

Name: ____

Age: ____

Nationality: ____

Socioeconomic Level as a child: _____________________

Socioeconomic Level as an adult: ____________________

Hometown: ____

Occupation: ____

Talents/Skills: _____________________________________

Siblings (describe relationship): ___________________

____

____

Spouse (describe relationship): _____________________

Children (describe relationship): ___________________

____

____

Grandparents (describe relationship): _______________

____

____

Grandchildren (describe relationship): ______________

____

____

Significant Others (describe relationship): _________

____

____

Relationship skills: ________________________________

PHYSICAL CHARACTERISTICS:

Height: ____

Weight: ____

Race: ____

Eye Color: ____

Hair Color: ____

Glasses or contact lenses? _________________________________

Skin color: ____

Shape of Face: ____

Distinguishing features: ___________________________________

How does he/she dress? ___________________________________

Mannerisms: ____

Habits (smoking, drinking etc.): ____________________________

Health: ____

Hobbies: ____

Favorite Sayings: ____

Disabilities: ____

Style: ____

INTELLECTUAL/MENTAL/PERSONALITY ATTRIBUTES AND ATTITUDES

Educational Background: ___________________________________

Any Mental Illnesses? _____________________________________

Character's short-term goals in life: _________________________

Character's long-term goals in life: _________________________

How does Character see himself/herself? _____________________

____

How does Character believe he/she is perceived by others? _______

____

How self-confident is the character? _________________________

Does the character seem ruled by emotion or logic or some combination thereof? ______

____

____

EMOTIONAL CHARACTERISTICS

Strengths/Weaknesses: ____________________________________

Introvert or Extrovert? ____________________________________

How does the character deal with anger? _____________________

With sadness? ____
With conflict? ____
With change? ____
With loss? ____
What would the character change about him/her-self? ____________________
What motivates this character? ____
What are this character's main personality traits? ______________________

____
____
____

SPIRITUAL CHARACTERISTICS

Does the character believe in God? ______________________________________
What are the character's spiritual beliefs? ______________________________
Is religion or spirituality a part of this character's life? ______________
If so, what role does it play? ____

How the Character is Involved in the Story

Character's role in the novel (main character? hero? heroine? Romantic interest? etc.):

____
Scene where character first appears: ____________________________________

____

Relationships with other characters: (Describe relationship with the following characters)
1. *Name*: ______________________________ *Relationship*: ________________

____
____

2. *Name*: ______________________________ *Relationship*: ________________

____
____

3. *Name*: ______________________________ *Relationship*: ________________

____

____

4. *Name*: _________________________________ *Relationship*: ____________________________

____

____

5. *Name*: _________________________________ *Relationship*: ____________________________

____

____

How is this character different at the end of the novel from when the novel began:

____

____

____

____

____

____

____

____

Additional Notes on This Character:

____

____

____

____

____

____

____

____

____

____

____

Character Profile Worksheet

<table>
<tr><td>PICK ONE</td></tr>
<tr><td>____ Protagonist</td></tr>
<tr><td>____ Antagonist</td></tr>
<tr><td>____ Supporting Character</td></tr>
</table>

Character #10 Name: _______________________________________

BASIC STATISTICS CHARACTER #10

Name: _______________________________________

Age: _______________________________________

Nationality: _______________________________________

Socioeconomic Level as a child: _______________________________________

Socioeconomic Level as an adult: _______________________________________

Hometown: _______________________________________

Occupation: _______________________________________

Talents/Skills: _______________________________________

Siblings (describe relationship): _______________________________________

____

____

Spouse (describe relationship): _______________________________________

Children (describe relationship): _______________________________________

____

____

Grandparents (describe relationship): _______________________________________

____

____

Grandchildren (describe relationship): _______________________________________

____

____

Significant Others (describe relationship): _______________________________________

____

____

Relationship skills: _______________________________________

PHYSICAL CHARACTERISTICS:

Height: _______________________________________

Weight: _______________________________________

Race: ____

Eye Color: ____

Hair Color: ____

Glasses or contact lenses? ____

Skin color: ____

Shape of Face: ____

Distinguishing features: ____

How does he/she dress? ____

Mannerisms: ____

Habits (smoking, drinking etc.): _____________________________________

Health: ____

Hobbies: ____

Favorite Sayings: ____

Disabilities: ____

Style: ____

INTELLECTUAL/MENTAL/PERSONALITY ATTRIBUTES AND ATTITUDES

Educational Background: ____

Any Mental Illnesses? ____

Character's short-term goals in life: _________________________________

Character's long-term goals in life: __________________________________

How does Character see himself/herself? _______________________________

____

How does Character believe he/she is perceived by others? _____________

____

How self-confident is the character? __________________________________

Does the character seem ruled by emotion or logic or some combination thereof? _______

____

____

EMOTIONAL CHARACTERISTICS

Strengths/Weaknesses: ____

Introvert or Extrovert? ____

How does the character deal with anger? _______________________________

With sadness? ____

With conflict? ____

With change? ____

With loss? ____

What would the character change about him/her-self? _____________________

What motivates this character? ____

What are this character's main personality traits? _______________________

____

____

____

SPIRITUAL CHARACTERISTICS

Does the character believe in God? _______________________________________

What are the character's spiritual beliefs? _______________________________

Is religion or spirituality a part of this character's life? __________________

If so, what role does it play? ____

How the Character is Involved in the Story

Character's role in the novel (main character? hero? heroine? Romantic interest? etc.):

____

Scene where character first appears: _____________________________________

____

____

Relationships with other characters: (Describe relationship with the following characters)

1. *Name*: ___________________________ *Relationship*: ___________________

____

____

2. *Name*: ___________________________ *Relationship*: ___________________

____

____

3. *Name*: ___________________________ *Relationship*: ___________________

____

____

4. *Name*: _______________________ *Relationship*: _______________________

____

____

5. *Name*: _______________________ *Relationship*: _______________________

____

____

How is this character different at the end of the novel from when the novel began:

____

____

____

____

____

____

____

____

Additional Notes on This Character:

____

____

____

____

____

____

____

____

____

____

____

CHARACTER DEVELOPMENT LETTER EXERCISE

Character #1   Name: _______________________________________

Write a letter, from Character #1, to you or any other character. This letter should be open, honest, and revealing. NOTE: This exercise can be completed at any time throughout the brainstorming/planning process.

Write a letter, from Character #2, to you or any other character. This letter should be open, honest, and revealing. NOTE: This exercise can be completed at any time throughout the brainstorming/planning process.

Character #3 Name: ____

Write a letter, from Character #3, to you or any other character. This letter should be open, honest, and revealing. NOTE: This exercise can be completed at any time throughout the brainstorming/planning process.

Character #4   Name: ____

Write a letter, from Character #4, to you or any other character. This letter should be open, honest, and revealing. NOTE: This exercise can be completed at any time throughout the brainstorming/planning process.

Character #5 Name: ____

Write a letter, from Character #5, to you or any other character. This letter should be open, honest, and revealing. NOTE: This exercise can be completed at any time throughout the brainstorming/planning process.

Write a letter, from Character #6, to you or any other character. This letter should be open, honest, and revealing. NOTE: This exercise can be completed at any time throughout the brainstorming/planning process.

Character #7   Name: ____

Write a letter, from Character #7, to you or any other character. This letter should be open, honest, and revealing. NOTE: This exercise can be completed at any time throughout the brainstorming/planning process.

Character #8 Name: _______________________________________

Write a letter, from Character #8, to you or any other character. This letter should be open, honest, and revealing. NOTE: This exercise can be completed at any time throughout the brainstorming/planning process.

Character #9   Name: ____

Write a letter, from Character #9, to you or any other character. This letter should be open, honest, and revealing. NOTE: This exercise can be completed at any time throughout the brainstorming/planning process.

Character #10   Name: ____

Write a letter, from Character #10, to you or any other character. This letter should be open, honest, and revealing. NOTE: This exercise can be completed at any time throughout the brainstorming/planning process.

Scene Development

OK, you've already developed your skeleton outline and worked on some character development, now we are going to tackle some scene development. By looking at your skeleton outline you should be able to get a rough idea of the order your scenes should come in, but don't worry you don't have to be committed to it just yet. Use the Scene Brainstorming Exercise blocks on the next few pages to jot down everything you already know about the story. It doesn't matter if you know where in the story each scene will be, right now it's all about remembering and recording all of the ideas you have about the story right now. This is an UNSTRUCTURED and UNCENSORED exercise, so don't hold back!

Scene Brainstorming Exercise

Use the scene brainstorming blocks below to brainstorm ideas for individual scenes. Without actually writing the manuscript text, write down as much as you know about each scene: the setting, which characters are involved, any conflict, conflict resolution, dialogue if it comes to you, etc.

Setting: ____

Characters: ____

Conflict:

____

Resolution: ____

Brainstorm:

____

____

____

____

____

____

____

____

Setting: ____

Characters: ____

Conflict:

____

Resolution: ____

Brainstorm:

____

____

____

____

____

____

____

____

Setting: ____

Characters: ____

Conflict: ____

Resolution: ____

Brainstorm:

____

____

____

____

____

____

____

Setting: ____

Characters: ____

Conflict: ____

Resolution: ____

Brainstorm:

____
____
____
____
____
____
____
____

Setting: ____

Characters: ____

Conflict: ____

Resolution: ____

Brainstorm:

____
____
____
____
____
____
____

Setting: ____

Characters: ____

Conflict: ____

Resolution: ____

Brainstorm:

____

____

____

____

____

____

____

____

Setting: ____

Characters: ____

Conflict: ____

Resolution: ____

Brainstorm:

____

____

____

____

____

____

____

Setting: ____

Characters: ____

Conflict: ____

Resolution: ____

Brainstorm:

____
____
____
____
____
____
____

Setting: ____

Characters: ____

Conflict: ____

Resolution: ____

Brainstorm:

____
____
____
____
____
____

Setting: ____

Characters: ____

Conflict: ____

Resolution: ____

Brainstorm:

____

____

____

____

____

____

____

____

Setting: ____

Characters: ____

Conflict: ____

Resolution: ____

Brainstorm:

____

____

____

____

____

____

____

Setting: ____

Characters: ____

Conflict: ____

Resolution: ____

Brainstorm:

____

____

____

____

____

____

____

____

Setting: ____

Characters: ____

Conflict: ____

Resolution: ____

Brainstorm:

____

____

____

____

____

____

____

Setting: ____

Characters: ____

Conflict: ____

Resolution: ____

Brainstorm:

____

____

____

____

____

____

____

____

Setting: ____

Characters: ____

Conflict: ____

Resolution: ____

Brainstorm:

____

____

____

____

____

____

____

____

Setting Development

The setting of your story is going to give your readers a backdrop to the visuals you create through your scenes. That means, you have to know everything about where your story takes place and the environment you're going to create for your characters. Is the setting based on a childhood memory, the diner you frequent, the city you live in? Is the setting on of a grand scale like the worlds created in Star Wars, The Lord of the Rings, or Game of Thrones? Is it a single location like in Misery, Cube, Clerks, or The Breakfast Club? You need to answer these questions before you move onto the next phase. The next exercise is to brainstorm everything you know about your setting. EVERYTHING – even if you don't think its relevant to the story.

Setting Brainstorming Exercise

Don't restrict yourself during this exercise and feel free to come back and add to your list anytime. Like all of these exercises, the more you learn about your characters, the setting, and the story, the more you will want to revise what you thought you knew.

Story Development

This is the final step before you'll begin the typing process. I call it story development because what you're going to create is essentially the full story layout. If you've ever worked in film, you might recognize this as a form of story boarding. Where this style differs from regular story boarding, is the addition of a detailed story outline process.

Story Development Exercise

There is no ideal number of scenes for a book, you might have fifteen you might have fifty. Often times the length of a book is determined by the genera you're writing in. There is a lot of information on the internet discussing the typical book/novel lengths by genera. If you have questions, I recommend doing a little research in that area. However, as long as you have enough scenes to tell your story without dragging it on unnecessarily, the number doesn't really matter.

In each of the 3-box scene story boarding panels below, you will draw out – if your creative – or jot down details of each scene's beginning, middle, and end. This should be done in chronological order, or your stories cover to cover order if not chronological. In the lines below each set of story boarding blocks, you'll write in more detail about what happens in each scene. The written description should be no more than two or three sentences.

SCENE #1

SCENE #2

SCENE #3

SCENE #4

SCENE #5

SCENE #6

SCENE #7

SCENE #8

SCENE #9

SCENE #12

SCENE #13

SCENE #14

SCENE #15

SCENE #16

SCENE #17

SCENE #18

SCENE #19

SCENE #20

SCENE #21

SCENE #22

SCENE #23

SCENE #24

SCENE #25

SCENE #26

SCENE #27

Time to Type

By now, you're probably eager to get started and at this point, you should have more than enough details about your characters and your story to begin your first draft. Don't worry about editing as you go, just open Microsoft Word—or your program of choice—and start typing. My suggestion is to start with scene one, from your story development exercise, and add the missing details and character dialogue. Each scene, at least to start, will be a chapter of its own. As you add more and more detail you may find that each scene evolves into more than just a single chapter or that some scenes can be merged together. If your finding it hard to work in a scene, move on to the next scene. You can always come back and tie scenes together later. Writer's block is real, you'll find suggestions on how to deal with it later in this guide.

Every time you sit down to write you'll want to review your outline, and read the notes for the scene you're about to work on. If at some point, and it will happen, you are struck with an idea that isn't in your notes—but you love it—go with it. Writing is art, it shouldn't be censored. Let your imagination run free and listen to your characters, they will tell you where the story is supposed to go.

Timeline Tracker

Use this section to keep track of your stories timeline, important events, etc. by adding in the information as you go.

CHAPTER NUMBER:	SETTING	DATE/TIME PERIOD	IMPORTANT EVENT	NOTES
1				
2				
3				
4				
5				
6				

CHAPTER NUMBER:	SETTING	DATE/TIME PERIOD	IMPORTANT EVENT	NOTES
7				
8				
9				
10				
11				
12				
13				
14				
15				
16				
17				
18				
19				

CHAPTER NUMBER:	SETTING	DATE/TIME PERIOD	IMPORTANT EVENT	NOTES
20				
21				
22				
23				
24				
25				
26				
27				
28				
29				
30				
31				
32				

"Description begins in the writer's imagination, but should finish in the reader's."
- Stephen King

Future Story Ideas

The truth is, most writers—myself included—often have more than one project going at a time. They might be in the writing process for one, the editing stage for another, and just brainstorming a number of other ideas. That can be a lot of information to try and keep straight. So, use the following section to journal those random story ideas while they are still fresh in your mind. Then, when you're ready, pick up another copy of this outlining and planning guide and get started on your next novel.

Working Title: ____

Genre: ____

Project Notes:

Working Title: ____

Genre: ____

Project Notes:

Working Title: ____

Genre: ____

Project Notes:

____

____

____

____

____

____

____

____

____

____

____

____

____

____

____

____

____

____

____

____

____

Working Title: ____

Genre: ____

Project Notes:

____

____

____

____

____

____

____

____

____

____

____

____

____

____

____

____

____

____

____

____

____

____

Working Title: ____

Genre: ____

Project Notes:

Working Title: ____

Genre: ____

Project Notes:

____

____

____

____

____

____

____

____

____

____

____

____

____

____

____

____

____

____

____

____

____

Working Title: ____

Genre: ____

Project Notes:

____

____

____

____

____

____

____

____

____

____

____

____

____

____

____

____

____

____

____

____

____

____

____

____

Dealing with Writer's Block

At some point, all writers experience writer's block. It isn't fun and it can make you question why you're even trying. The thing is, you just have to push through! Below I've listed some suggestions for getting through those hard times. Not every idea will work for every writer, which is why I have so many choices, but through trial and error you should be able to find one or two that work for you.

1. **Step away** – Take a fifteen-minute walk, preferably outside, to help clear your mind.
2. **Read a book** – A good author is always reading, so look at it as research!
3. **Journal** – Free writing about anything but your story is a great way to distract your mind.
4. **Eliminate distractions** – Turn off the tv, shut the door, whatever it takes.
5. **Change your environment** – Sometimes sitting at a desk staring at a computer screen can block creativity all on its own. Grab a pen and paper and head outside to brainstorm the scene you're working on. The change in scenery and the change in writing medium can help push you past what's blocking you.
6. **Listen to music** – Are you the type of person who needs a little ambient noise? Find music that fits the theme of your story and let it play softly in the background.
7. **Grab a drink** – Whatever your drink of choice, I don't judge. I love writing with a stemming hot cup of coffee in the morning, afternoon, or evening. However, when I'm working on a serious scene, red wine hits the spot!
8. **Bond** – Spend some one-on-one time with your significant other, your kids, or just a good friend and focus on them – not you – not what your writing – them. Sometimes just getting out of your own head and into someone else's can spark new and exciting ideas.
9. **Surf the web** – Normally I would say surfing the internet while writing is a distraction that can lead to lots of lost time, but if you're experiencing writer's block, the internet can be a great source of information to pull your focus away from what is blocking you and back to a more creative mindset.
10. **Meditate** – Ten minutes of quiet, deep breathing time can do wonders for focus. This is probably one of my favorite ways to deal with, and prevent, writer's block. I meditate ten to twenty minutes a day, often times right before I start writing, and have found that it significantly decreases my writer's block. If you want help with meditation – maybe your new to it – check out my self-help meditation guide *The Invisible You*, available on amazon in paperback.

"You don't write because you want to
say something. You write because you
have something to say."
- F. Scott Fitzgerald

<u>Self-Publishing 101</u>

This book isn't about publishing your manuscript, but I also don't want to leave you in the dark once you finish that first draft. So, very briefly, below is the Self-Publishing Checklist I use:

X	Task	Estimated Completion Time	When to Complete
	Research and finalize the manuscript's title		As early as possible
	Write book description for marketing		As early as possible
	Write back cover copy		As early as possible
	Send final manuscript (after initial re-writes) to beta readers	2-4 weeks	4.5 months prior to publication date
	Review beta reader notes, rewrite and resolve all issues	1-2 weeks	3.5 months prior to publication date
	Send final manuscript to copyeditor (HIRE a copyeditor – this is not where you want to skimp on money)	2-4 weeks	3 months prior to publication date
	Hire a cover design artist (send book description and notes on cover design) or design yourself if you are artistic	2-4 weeks	3 months prior to publication date
	Start online/social media marketing campaign	3 months	3 months prior to publication date
	Review the copyedit and resolve all issues	1-2 weeks	2 months prior to publication date
	Finalize the front cover design		2 months prior to publication date
	(For Print Version) Create design element list for interior		2 months prior to publication date
	(For Print Version) Send final copy to interior designer – IF NOT DOING THIS YOURSELF		2 months prior to publication date
	Write your author bio, dedication, and acknowledgements		2 months prior to publication date
	(For Print Version) Review designed pages; adjust/revise	1-2 weeks	1 month prior to publication date
	(For Print Version) Complete back cover design and Spine (If you hired a cover artist, they should have done this too)	1-2 weeks	1 month prior to publication date
	(For Digital Version) Create EPUB/MOBI Files – Very simple if using an online self-publishing company like KDP	Varies by process used.	2-4 weeks prior to publication date
	Proofread final files in all formats, make edits/formatting adjustments as needed.	1-2 weeks	1-2 weeks prior to publication date

Notes Pages

<u>Notes Pages</u>

Notes Pages

Notes Pages

Notes Pages

About the Author

Nina has always been creative, be it art, theatre, film – anything but singing – you don't want to hear that! She earned her bachelor's degree in Theatre and Military Science from Eastern Michigan University where she spent most of her time either on stage, rappelling down buildings, or working one of three jobs. After college she moved to Los Angeles, like so many other actors, in pursuit of her dreams. Nina started writing short stories in 2008. Since then, her dreams have gotten bigger and according to her kids, her storytelling ability has gotten better. She has done everything from secretarial work to business development to being the Director of a private preschool. She has fired a M16 machine gun, jumped out of a C130 aircraft, and given birth – TWICE - but she always returns to her art. Since publishing her first novel Awaken, the first book in the Blood Angel Series, in 2012 she hasn't stopped writing.

Though she'll forever be a Michigan girl at heart, she now lives in the warmth of the south with her husband and two beautiful children. If she's not working on her latest story, you can find her lounging with a good book, playing with her kids, or indulging in her unhealthy addiction to Starbucks coffee.

Other Books by Nina Soden

The Blood Angel Series ~ Young Adult Fiction

- Awaken (book 1)
- Beginnings (book 2)
- Revenge (book 3)
- Pursuit (book 4)

The SECTOR C Series ~ Young Adult Fiction

- The Chosen (book 1)
- The Hunted (book 2)
- Book 3 coming soon

The Invisible You ~ 52 Weeks of Meditations, Activities, and Writing Prompts to Help You Discover YOU!